TOPICS
IN HOME
ECONOMICS

FOOD CHOICE

Anita Tull

Oxford University Press 1986

Oxford University Press, Walton Street, Oxford OX2 6DP

Oxford New York Toronto
Delhi Bombay Calcutta Madras Karachi
Petaling Jaya Singapore Hong Kong Tokyo
Nairobi Dar es Salaam Cape Town Melbourne Auckland

and associated companies in
Beirut Ibadan Berlin Nicosia

Oxford is a trade mark of Oxford University Press.

© Oxford University Press 1986
Reprinted 1987
ISBN 0 19 832721 8

Acknowledgements

Designed by Raynor Design.

Illustrations are by Gecko Ltd, Jon Riley and Kate Simunek.

The cover illustration is by Barbara Mullarney-Wright.

The publisher would like to thank the following for permission to reproduce their photographs:
BBC Hulton Picture Library p.30 (left); Flour Milling and Baking Research Association p.45; Format Photographers Ltd. p.9, p.15 (left and right), p.17, p.32 (left); Sally and Richard Greenhill p.10 (left); The John Hillelson Agency Ltd. p.16; Imperial War Museum p.13 (left and right); Bob Judges p.18, p.26, p.44; Steven Lee p.29; Jorge Lewinski p.10 (right); Network Photographers p.28 (left and right), p.32 (right); Royal College of Surgeons of England p.47 (left and right); Nicholas Tull p.24 (all); Wrighton International p.30 (right).

Set by Tradespools Ltd, Frome, Somerset
Printed in Great Britain
by Scotprint Ltd, Musselburgh

Contents

Part I—What influences food choice?

Introduction 4
History of food 5
Food from abroad 8
Religious beliefs and customs 10
Availability of food 12
Staple foods 14
Shortage of food 16
The cost of food 18
Likes and dislikes 20
The senses (1) 22
The senses (2) 24
Advertising 26
Food technology 28
Facilities for storing and preparing food 30

Part II—How food choice affects health

Food and health 32
The nutrients 34
Individual needs for food 36
Dietary goals 38
Thinking about sugar 40
Thinking about fat 42
Thinking about fibre 44
Thinking about salt 46
Thinking about alcohol 47
Heart disease 48
Being overweight 52
Dental disease and intestinal disease 54
Low sugar recipes 56
Low fat recipes 58
High fibre recipes 60
Quiz—what sort of food chooser are you? 62
Index 64

Part I

What influences food choice?

Introduction

What did you have to eat yesterday?
Why did you choose those foods? Did you have a choice?
Many people take food for granted, especially when there is plenty of it available. Perhaps you have never thought about why you choose to eat certain foods and not others.

There are many reasons why we choose to eat some foods and not others. This book looks at the factors that influence what people eat. Many people in the world do not have a choice of food because they do not have enough; this is considered too.

Food also affects health, and often people do not make the best choices for their health. With this in mind, this book aims to help people make a more careful and considered choice of food.

History of food

We can go back in time to find out the type of food eaten and how it was grown, collected, and prepared. There is a lot of information available ranging from drawings to historic recipe books.

Half a million years ago

People had to search and had to eat what they could find, for example roots, fruit, eggs, and insects. They made simple tools to collect food and to kill animals. When people discovered how to make fire they were able to eat a wider range of foods which were too tough to eat when raw. This was the beginning of the art of cooking and roasting food over a fire was the main method.

4000 BC

All the basic cooking methods (boiling, baking, stewing, etc.) were used. People settled down in one place, and started to keep animals such as cattle and sheep in herds. They cultivated (ploughed, watered, and weeded) the land, and grew grain (cereals). Oxen were used to pull wooden ploughs through the soil.

2000 BC

The Ancient Britons discovered how to make the metal bronze from tin and copper. They made arrows, axes, spears, and ploughs. It was easier to grow food and kill animals using bronze tools, than to use stone and wooden tools. The main crops they grew were wheat and barley, which were ground into a rough flour to make a coarse kind of bread.

50–100 AD

In 55 AD, the Romans came to Britain, and brought much useful knowledge with them about growing food. They organised marsh-draining, manuring, cultivation of orchards, and wheat-growing on a large scale. They kept bees, hens, and geese in large numbers and introduced a whole new range of foods, such as leeks, lettuces, beans, cauliflowers, sweet and spicy sauces, and peas.

500–800 AD

During this time, the Anglo Saxons lived in Britain. They settled in groups, farmed and traded in foods, metals, etc. People worked together to produce food. The Vikings then invaded Britain, and organised a feudal system. This was a system of landlords who collected rent from the peasants (called serfs), who farmed strips of land, on which they grew vegetables, some cereals, and kept livestock. Often the serfs had to pay their rent with the food which they produced, which meant that they had less to eat themselves.

800–1500 AD

During these centuries there was a big difference in the lifestyles of the rich and poor. Most people had only coarse bread, cheese, eggs, ale, fish, and sometimes meat, and a few vegetables to eat.

Wealthy people ate well, and often held exotic banquets. During this time the Crusaders brought back many spices, fruits, and vegetables from their travels to the East, and although these luxuries were expensive, they became popular.

1700–1900 AD

Poor people continued to eat very simply, and the rich ate very well. Tea and coffee became popular as importing got easier. After the onset of the Industrial Revolution, more people went to live in towns, so food had to be brought in from the countryside. Improvements were made in agricultural techniques, so that more food could be produced. Many people, however, could not afford to buy sufficient food.

The 20th century

This century has seen great improvements in the distribution of food to all members of society. Most people can afford to eat well, and the standard of food hygiene and production has greatly improved. Research into agriculture and food technology continues, so that more and new types of food can be produced, but there are still many people in the world who go hungry.

▷ **Things to do**

1 Choose a period of history, and find out more about the food that was grown and eaten in that time. Present your work as a wall display or project. Make up a menu for a meal that would have been eaten, and describe how it would have been cooked.
2 Before shops became common, how was food sold and bought?
3 List all the problems you can think of that people who had to grow their own food (such as the serfs in Viking times) would have had to deal with, and the effects these would have had on their lives.
4 Before food hygiene laws came into being, food was often 'adulterated' so that the seller could make a bigger profit. Find out what this means, and give some examples of what happened, and the effects this had on the people who bought and ate the adulterated food. ◁

Food from abroad

The choice of food available in the UK has increased greatly in recent years. We now import many different and unusual types of food from a variety of countries. For example, lychees, which are grown in China and other parts of Asia, the USA, and Australia, are available in the summer in the UK. They are small fruits, about the size of cherries. They have a thin shell, and white flesh tinged with pink. They have the texture of a soft grape and a delicate flavour. They are eaten raw or poached gently in syrup. Lychees can also be bought in tins. They are used in fruit salads and in sweet chicken and duck dishes in Chinese cooking.

▷ Below is a list of imported foods now available in the UK. Choose four, and find out what they are, where they come from, and what they are used for. You can find the information in reference books, leaflets from some supermarkets, some recipe books, or on packets and labels. ◁

kiwi fruit	water chestnuts	capsicums
yams	basmati rice	garam masala
ladies fingers (okra)	tagliatelle	bean sprouts
Chinese cabbage	gnocci	passion fruit
mung beans	popadoms	

Now that travel abroad is popular and easy, people are able to try traditional foods from other countries. Some of these traditional dishes have become popular in the UK. For example, minestrone is a filling soup from northern Italy. It is often served as a main meal. It contains a variety of fresh vegetables, pulses (beans, lentils), rice or spaghetti, bacon or ham, and herbs such as basil or marjoram. Parmesan cheese is sprinkled on top, and it is served with crusty rolls and Chianti, which is a popular Italian red wine.

An Italian meal

Lychees

▷ Below is a list of traditional dishes from a variety of countries. Choose six, and find out where they come from, what are the main ingredients in each, and what each is served with. ◁

black forest gateau	dolmades	angel cake
ratatouille	shish kebab	gazpacho
coq au vin	taramasalata	savarin
paella	beef stroganoff	croissants
goulash	dhal	beef vindaloo
apfelstrudel	chow mein	moussaka

Many foreign restaurants have opened in the UK, which enable people to try a wider choice of food without having to travel far.

People from many different countries, such as India, the West Indies, and China, have come to live permanently in the UK. They generally continue to eat traditional meals from their own countries, and in order to provide suitable ingredients, many new shops have opened in areas where there are different ethnic groups. This has widened food choice as unusual types of spices, fruits, and vegetables can often be purchased.

▷ **Things to do**

1 Make a list of the types and numbers of foreign restaurants and take-away shops in the town nearest to you. If you cannot visit the town, then look them up under 'restaurants' in the local yellow pages telephone directory.
2 Which types of restaurant seem to be the most popular? Why do you think this is? If possible, visit a few of them and look at the menus they have (usually displayed in the window), and make a list of some of the foods they have on offer.
3 It is possible to buy ready prepared foods that need very little cooking (convenience foods), and some of these are in the form of meals from abroad. Look round a food shop and make a list of those that are available, their price, and how they are prepared at home. ◁

Religious beliefs and customs

Religious beliefs have great importance in the lives of many people and in some cases influence what they choose to eat. Often, religions have special laws or instructions about what should and should not be eaten. Many ceremonies, for example marriages, funerals, and days of religious importance are celebrated by either a **feast** or a **fast** (going without food for a specific length of time).

There are many religious beliefs associated with food. Examples from the four most well known religions are included here:

The Christian faith

There are two main festive seasons in this faith—Easter and Christmas, when traditional foods are prepared and eaten. These festivals are also celebrated by many people who are not regular church attenders.

Harvest festivals in the late summer are often celebrated with special suppers. Also churches and schools often collect food and distribute it to people in need. Some people fast by replacing meat with fish on Fridays. Some give up an item of food during the season of Lent.

A Christmas meal   A Jewish sabbath

The Jewish faith

The old testament of the bible (Leviticus chapter 11) sets out Jewish food customs and dietary laws. Those foods that fulfil the requirements of the Jewish law are called **Kosher foods**. Only the meat of cud-chewing, cloven-footed animals (listed in Deuteronomy chapter 16) may be eaten: beef, lamb, and venison. Only clean birds, as stated in the Talmud (a collection of writings including law and legend), may be eaten. Scavengers and unclean birds of prey are forbidden. Foods which are forbidden include: pork, bacon, ham, shellfish, eels, eggs with blood spots, and gelatine. There are also laws which specify that milk and meat should not be eaten or prepared together, which some strict (orthodox) Jews may follow.

The sabbath day (sunset on Friday to sunset on Saturday) is celebrated with a special meal which all the family attend. Many Jewish festivals are celebrated with special meals, for example, the Passover.

The Hindu faith

Hindus will not kill cows for food as they are considered to be sacred. The cow is important because of the work it does in ploughing the land to grow food. They will, however, eat products from the cow (milk, butter, and sometimes cheese) because the cow is not killed to make these. Pigs are not eaten because they are regarded as unclean. Some Hindus will not eat any animal food which has caused the animal to be killed.

The Muslim faith

Some of the laws the Muslims follow are similar to the Jewish ones, for example they do not eat pigs. Other animals have to be ritually slaughtered, a process known as **Halal**. Some Muslims do eat fish. During Ramadan (the main fast of Islam), which lasts for one month every year, many strict Muslims do not eat or drink anything between sunrise and sunset. Meals therefore take place at night.

Food customs

Some festive occasions are not based on religious laws, but have a social or ritual importance that has very little to do with the nutritional value of the foods involved. Two examples are New Year and Guy Fawkes night in the UK. Other countries have their own special festive occasions too.

▷ **Things to do**

1 Choose one of the four religious faiths above, or any other religion, and find out more details about the actual foods that are eaten in special meals. Present your findings in the form of a wall chart which could be displayed with others to teach people about the beliefs of different groups of people.
2 Find out and write down the origins of the following food customs:
   pancake day (Shrove Tuesday)
   Mothers' day cake
   mince pies at Christmas
   mint sauce eaten with lamb ◁

Availability of food

A visit to any large supermarket in the UK shows something which people take very much for granted—that there is no shortage of food here. Large supermarkets stock hundreds of different types and brands of food in fresh and preserved forms. Many bake bread on the premises and have their own butchers and fresh fish departments where the goods are prepared for sale.

Many foods are **imported** from other countries. In 1980, the UK imported £5.6 billion worth of food and exported £2.9 billion worth. In the same year, £29 billion worth of food was eaten in the UK, and much of this was produced here.

If a country is able to produce all the food it needs, it is said to be **self sufficient**. However, many countries cannot produce all they need for various reasons, including:

a poor climate—for example one that is too wet, too dry, too cold
insufficient land
unsuitable land for growing food—for example desert, mountains
lack of money to buy the latest agricultural machinery and technology

What do we import?

These are some of the items the UK imported in 1980:

£359 million worth of bacon and ham
£245 million worth of canned meats
£116 million worth of fresh vegetables
£113 million worth of processed and preserved fruit
£101 million worth of fresh tomatoes
 £96 million worth of processed vegetables
 £35 million worth of beer
  £9 million worth of oats and rye

We import much bacon and ham from countries like Denmark because they are able to produce these foods more cheaply than we can and because of trading agreements between the two countries.

▷ Make a list of countries from which we import the foods listed above. To help you, look at the labels and packets of the foods; the country of origin is usually printed there. ◁

Rationing food

Food has not always been in plentiful supply in Britain. During the First and Second World Wars there was a great shortage of food.

In the First World War, many people nearly starved because food was not fairly distributed and many could not afford to buy it.

In the Second World War, the Ministry of Food and the Ministry of Agriculture and Fisheries made sure that food was strictly **rationed**, and people were given ration books which contained tokens that they exchanged for food. The list below shows the weekly food ration for one person in 1942:

Meat   1 lb (offal, fish, and poultry not rationed but limited)
Cheese   3 oz
Bacon and ham   4 oz
Tea   2 oz
Sugar   8 oz
Preserves   4 oz of jam or marmalade, or syrup
Fats   2 oz butter, 4 oz margarine, 2 oz cooking fat
Eggs   1 fresh every other week, some dried egg available
Milk   2 pints

It was nearly impossible to buy citrus fruits (oranges, lemons, etc.) and bananas, and people were encouraged to 'Dig for Victory' and grow their own fruit and vegetables. It was not possible to buy frozen foods and very difficult to obtain items like rice and pasta which had to be imported. Sweets were also very strictly rationed. Food was still rationed until 1954, nine years after the war ended.

▷ **Things to do**

1 Study the list of rationed foods above, and plan a weeks meals for one person using those foods, plus fruit and vegetables (remember—not imported ones), flour, and bread. Afterwards, discuss how difficult or easy this was, and the problems people may have had during the war. Remember that as fruit and vegetables were grown in the UK only, they would be restricted to particular seasons. For example, root vegetables tend to be winter vegetables, whilst tomatoes and lettuces are summer ones.

2 It is often said that people were healthier during the war because of the food rationing. Why do you think this was so? ◁

Staple foods

The staple food for a group of people is the main one grown in the area in which they live. It generally provides a large part of their daily food intake, and so is very important.

Cereal foods are the main staple foods throughout the world, as they are relatively cheap and easy to grow, provide a good supply of energy and nutrients, and are filling.

Rich countries, such as the UK, now use much of the cereals they grow to feed animals which are reared for meat or dairy products. Poor countries have to rely on cereals as their main food supply for the majority of their people.

The pictures below show the staple food (in bold) and other main foods eaten in some different countries:

As a country becomes more wealthy, it is able to import and grow a greater variety of foods, and so becomes less dependent on its staple food. People therefore have a greater choice, but often still continue to eat their staple food, though with a variety of other things. For example, many people in Europe eat bread (once the staple food) in large quantities, but tend to eat it with other foods, such as cheese, meat, and vegetables.

Not all staple foods are cereals of course. Eskimos in the Canadian Arctic eat mostly seal meat, as well as fish, birds, and eggs. They eat little plant foods. Californian Indians, who hunt and gather their food, eat acorns as their staple food, as well as grass, seeds, bulbs, berries, wild fruits, shellfish, deer, rabbits, and squirrels.

Cash crops

Many poor countries grow crops in large quantities to be exported to rich countries, in order to make money. These crops are often called cash crops, and they are not used to feed the population of the country, who may be in great need of food. Some examples of these cash crops are peanuts from Senegal and Gambia, cocoa from Western Nigeria, coffee from the Ivory Coast, and oil palm from South-eastern Nigeria.

Often the money earned from cash crops is used by a poor country to buy arms and weapons, especially if there is likely to be a war with a neighbouring country. This means that there is little, if any, money left for helping people to grow or buy food. Also if the demand for the cash crop in the rich countries goes down, the poor country will have no money for food, and famine results.

Cash crops from Uganda   A coffee plantation

▷ **Things to do**

1 Rice is the most important staple food—about half the world's population eat it as their main food. Using encyclopaedias and reference books, find out about the different varieties grown, how it is cultivated, and the various ways in which it is prepared for eating.
2 Find out what polished rice is, and why it is not as nutritional as wholegrain rice.
3 Find out which countries grow the following cash crops:
    sugar, tea, cotton, rubber, oranges ◁

Shortage of food

There are many countries where the choice of food is very limited, because it is in short supply. The word **famine** is used to describe the suffering which occurs due to a food shortage. There have been many famines in the past, for example the Irish Potato Famine in the 19th century, when many thousands of people died. The recent and very serious famine in Ethiopia demonstrates very tragically that the problems of famine are a long way from being prevented or solved.

Causes of famine

There are five main causes of famine:

1. **Crop destruction by pests and diseases** If the main crop in a country is attacked by insects, fungi, or other diseases, it can completely wipe out a whole year's supply of food.

▷ Find out what caused the Irish Potato Famine in the 19th Century. What are locusts? How do they affect food supplies, and which countries are often affected in this way? ◁

2. **Lack of water (drought)** Many countries with hot climates suffer from droughts which can go on year after year. Often the land is watered artificially from underground sources of water. This is called **irrigation**. If there is no irrigation, it becomes impossible to grow crops or feed livestock.

▷ Find out which countries in recent years have suffered famines as a result of droughts. ◁

3. **Natural disasters** Earthquakes, volcanic erruptions, and floods are a common threat in many countries. In a matter of minutes or hours, they can totally destroy crops, livestock, stores of food, and communication by road.

4. **War, civil unrest, and poverty** Lack of food is a common result of war. It may be impossible to transport food to everyone, and stores of food may be destroyed. Unfortunately in many countries at war there is no planning by the government to carefully ration food, and many people perish as a result.

Where there is extreme poverty (when people cannot afford to buy the essentials of life) famine is often the result. Sadly, this is a major cause of suffering in the world. It is estimated that as many as two-thirds of the world's population go hungry due to poverty, while the rest have too much.

5 **Population growth** Every second of the day and night, somewhere in the world, 4 babies are born. There were approximately 4 billion people in the world in 1976, and it is estimated that by the year 2000, there will be 6.5 billion. Improved health and medical care have lead to a drop in the death rate, particularly the infant death rate, which is one of the reasons for population growth. In many areas of the world, food production has barely kept up with this growth so that many people starve.

It is very easy to ignore the problems of famine, because we have little contact with it, except for what is broadcast on television and written about in the newspapers. It is difficult to imagine what it must be like to be literally starving when there is so much food available in the UK.

▷ **Things to do**

1 Study the photograph of these victims of famine and answer the questions below:
   a Why do the limbs become so weak?
   b Why do babies and children suffer so quickly in famines?
   c Why is disease such as cholera the ultimate cause of death for so many famine victims?

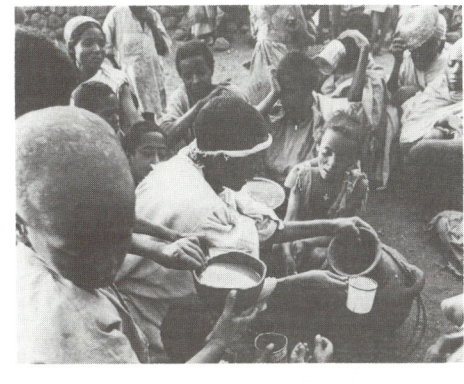

2 Many organizations—charities, churches, government bodies, try very hard to help people during a famine. Obviously the most important help they can give is to provide food. To do this they need money, donations of food, transport, and volunteers to organize and distribute the food.
   a Find out about some of the following organizations, and how they collect money and help for famines:
   Oxfam, Christian Aid, Save the Children, War on Want, The International Red Cross. You can find out about them by writing to their offices in this country (ask in a library or telephone directory enquiries for their addresses), or by looking them up in reference books in the library.
   b As a group, prepare a large visual display on the problems of famine—use information and pictures from books, newspapers, colour supplements, magazines, and literature from organizations like Oxfam.
   c Encourage people to come and look at your display. You may be able to combine this with a fund raising appeal in your school for famine victims. ◁

The cost of food

Everyone has to eat and so must spend part of their income (the money they have to live on) on food. The price of food is affected by many different factors, and the diagram below shows how some of these factors go together to make up the price of meat:

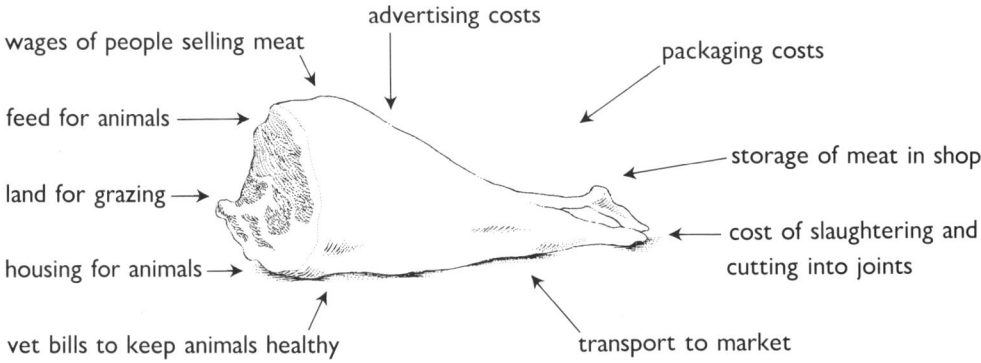

▷ Look at the foods below, and work out the factors that make up their costs. ◁

How does cost affect food choice?

Obviously, the more money a person has, the more food they are able to buy and the greater their choice. People who have plenty of money (a high income), can afford to have a large variety of meals and to eat out of the home in restaurants. For those with a small income, the choice is more limited, and it can be a hard task to buy enough food to meet with the needs, likes, and dislikes of a family.

It is possible to save money when shopping for food, in various ways:

a Buying foods that are in season—some foods, for example fruit and vegetables are cheaper at certain times of the year when they are at the peak of their growing season.
b Buying cheaper cuts of meat—some cuts of meat are tougher and therefore cheaper, for example shin of beef, breast of lamb, but with careful cooking can be made into tender and tasty meals.
c Comparing prices in different shops—obviously you have to have the time to do this, but it is often worth doing. Small independent shops tend to be more expensive than large supermarkets.

▷ Can you think of any other ways of saving money? ◁

▷ **Things to do**

1 Mrs. Brown is a widow, and lives alone. She only has £50 a week to live on. After she has paid for her rent, rates, heating, lighting, and other bills, she can only spare £15 a week for food. Mrs. Brown lives on the outskirts of a town, where there are a few local shops. She has to use public transport if she wants to go into town.

Work out a shopping list for Mrs. Brown to provide her with enough meals for a week. You will need to find out the prices of food by visiting a local food shop (a group could do this). To help you, here are a few facts about the type of meals Mrs. Brown likes:

Breakfast—she usually has cereal or toast with a cup of tea. Sometimes she likes to have fruit juice.
Midday meal—she prefers to have a main meal in the evening, so at this meal, Mrs. Brown has a light snack, for example soup and bread plus cake or fruit.
Evening meal—Mrs. Brown likes to have a two-course meal (main course and pudding), and enjoys cooking. She eats meat and fish, and quite likes offal (liver, kidney etc.). She enjoys fresh vegetables, and does not like too many fried foods.

2 Work out a shopping list in a similar way to **1** (above) for two students living on a grant, with £25 a week to spare for food for both of them. They have a canteen lunch at college which costs 60p each, five days a week, so you need to plan breakfasts and evening meals, and three meals a day at weekends with the remaining £19.

3 Different shops are often in competition with each other to attract customers. Make a list of ways in which shops try to persuade people to spend their money on food. ◁

Likes and dislikes

We eat to keep ourselves alive and healthy but most of us enjoy our food, especially if there is a large variety to choose from. In countries such as the UK and the USA, where there are many foods to choose from, people tend to eat foods they particularly like and avoid those which they dislike.

▷ Make a list of foods which you particularly like, and give a reason, for example you like the flavour, colour, texture.
Make a list of foods which you particularly dislike, and try to give a reason for each food. Some of your reasons may include:

1 You dislike the texture, flavour or colour.
2 You have never tried the food but do not like the look of it.
3 You associate the food with feeling ill.
4 You do not agree with the way in which the food is produced.
5 You do not like the food cooked in a particular way.

Some people are very choosy and eat only a small variety of foods. Such people can be very difficult to cater for. Look at your list of foods again—do you think you are too choosy? ◁

Restaurants, canteens, cafes, and other places where meals are sold have to provide a selection of foods for their customers to choose from, if they are to stay in business. This means that they must plan carefully.

Here are some menus from different restaurants and cafes. A menu should be clearly set out and explained to help a customer make a choice.

HONG KONG GARDEN
Chinese Restaurant & Take-away

Pork Dishes (served with rice)
Pork with black bean sauce £3.00
Pork with orange and garlic £2.70
Pork with beanshoots & mushrooms ... £2.70
Pork with mushrooms £2.50
Pork with sweet & sour sauce £2.70
Pork Chow Mein (noodles) £2.70
Pork Fu Yung (egg) £2.70

Extras
Fried Rice 70
Spring roll 50
Beanshoots 50

TRATTORIA ROMA

PASTA
Spaghetti bolognese £2.40
Spaghetti with seafood sauce £2.65
Lasagne £2.50
Canelloni £2.50
All served with salad & garlic bread

PIZZA
Pizza with cheese & tomato £2.70
Pizza with cheese & mushroom £2.80
Pizza with sausage £2.80
Pizza with anchovy & olives £2.80
Extra toppings 75p

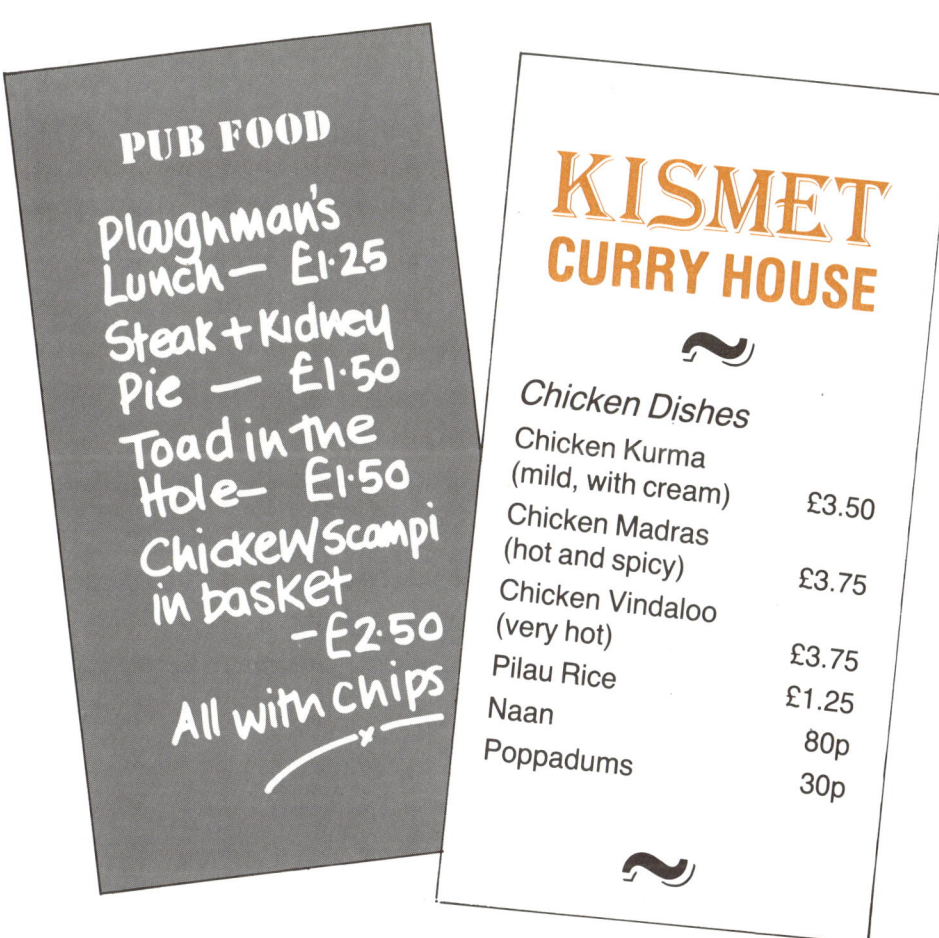

▷ **Things to do**

1 Imagine that you were asked to plan a menu for a small restaurant. Design and prepare such a menu using dishes you are most familiar with including starters, main courses, and sweets. Remember that your customers may not like everything that you offer, so give them a good choice.
2 You have been asked to help plan a five-year-old child's birthday party, where there will be twenty other children ranging from three to five years old. Plan the tea menu, remembering that small children get excited at parties and are quite likely to eat and drink a lot and can get quite messy in the process! Design some table decorations to make the party table attractive.
3 You have invited three friends to come and have an evening meal. One of them is a lacto vegetarian. Find out why some people are vegetarian and the sorts of foods that they do and do not eat. Plan a two-course menu for a meal that you can all enjoy. ◁

The senses (1)

We are able to detect what is going on around us because of special **sense organs**. These pick up information from outside the body and pass it to the brain. The brain then interprets the information so that the body can act accordingly. There are 5 senses, and 5 sense organs:

Sense	Sense organ
sight	the eyes
sound	the ears
touch	the skin
taste	the tongue
smell	the nose

Food provides us with **sensations**, for example aromas and flavours, which are detected by special nerves in the sense organs. All this happens in a fraction of a second. Our senses are at work even before we start to eat.

▷ Describe what happens if you pass a food shop or restaurant when you are hungry. What sensations would you feel? What would happen in your mouth? ◁

To enjoy food, the senses all work together; the senses of taste and smell in particular work very closely together.

Taste

Flavour is detected on the tongue by **taste buds**, which are found mainly on the edges and towards the back of the tongue.

The number of taste buds decreases with age so children are more sensitive to flavour than older people are.

Some taste buds react to only sweet, salt, sour (e.g. lemon juice), or bitter flavours. There are few bitter foods, but many poisonous things are bitter and would be rejected before they were swallowed. This helps to protect us from eating things that are poisonous. Some areas of the tongue are more sensitive than others to particular flavours as shown in the diagram opposite.

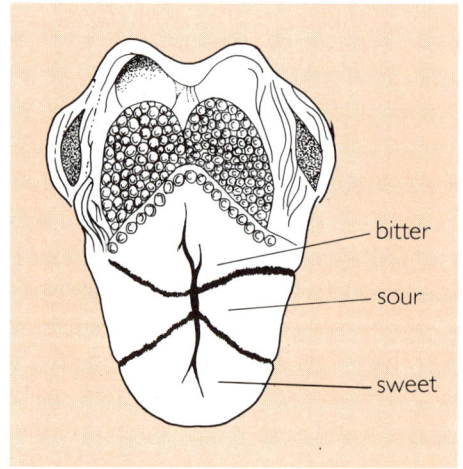

A human adult has approximately 10,000 taste buds on the tongue, and each of these consists of 15–20 **taste cells** arranged like the segments of an orange. The cells are constantly replaced as they die or become damaged—about every seven days.

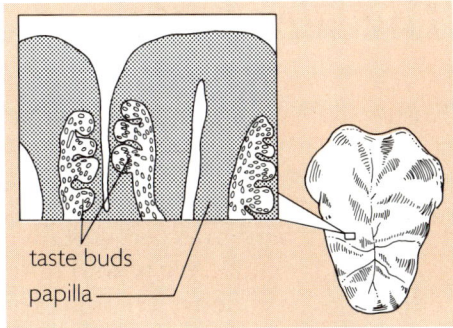

▷ Try the following experiment to find out about your taste buds. Close your eyes and get a friend to sprinkle separately some salt, sugar, and lemon juice or vinegar onto various parts of your tongue (which of course, you will have to stick out!). Copy the diagram of the tongue and show, by shading in different colours, which areas of your tongue were the most sensitive to those three items. Do your results agree with the diagram on page 22? ◁

Smell

There are special **receptor cells** lining the nasal passages which pick up aromas (smells) from the air, and nerves detect these chemical messages and send them to the brain. Our sense of smell is not as sensitive as that of other animals, but is important for the enjoyment of food and the recognition of many signals, e.g. danger.

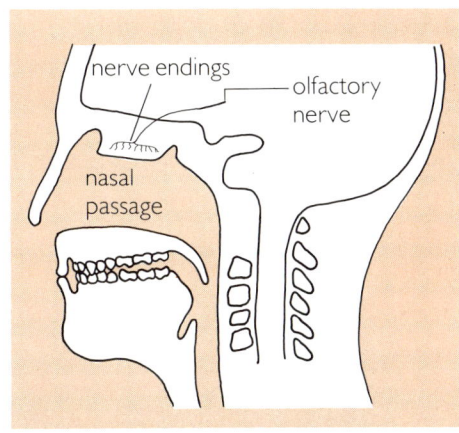

▷ **Things to do**

1 Try this experiment to show how the sense of smell and taste work together.
Collect various different foods—some common ones (salt, sugar, etc.), and some more unusual ones (green pepper, ginger, etc.). Give a small sample of each to a group of people who have closed their eyes and are pinching their noses shut. Ask them to identify the foods. Which foods were the most easy to identify?
Which foods were the most difficult to identify? Why was this?
2 Try the same experiment, but with a group of people who shut their eyes, but who do not pinch their noses. Compare the results. Is there any difference? Why do you think this is? ◁

The senses (2)

Sight

The way a food is presented has a great effect on our enjoyment of it. A meal may taste delicious, but if it is poorly served there will be no desire to eat it. We tend to expect certain foods to have a particular colour, shape, and texture. We would hesitate to choose a food if it did not meet with our expectations. Try this experiment.

▷ Collect some small amounts of fairly common foods, such as cooked rice, mashed potato, bread. Colour them with edible food colourings in an unusual way, for example blue potato, pink bread. Dilute the colouring in a little water, then mix it with a fork. Dip the bread in the colour then allow it to dry. Invite some friends to sample the foods (which should have normal flavours), and make a note of their reactions. ◁

Food manufacturers and people who prepare food in restaurants or hotels, are trained to present food in the most attractive and appetising way for their customers. Foods are often decorated before they are served—decorations on savoury foods are called **garnishes**, and include tomatoes, parsley, lemon slices, and toasted triangles. Sweet foods are decorated with things such as grated chocolate, cream, fruit, and chopped nuts. Sometimes the decorations on food are simple or they may be very elaborate—for example on a wedding cake.

▷ Look at the pictures below of foods that have not been 'finished off', and suggest how they can be made to look really appetising. ◁

Vegetable soup

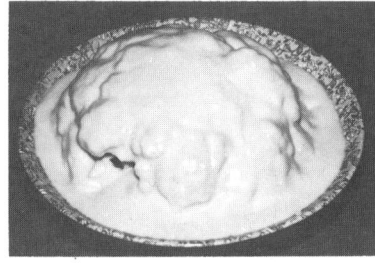
Cauliflower cheese

Chocolate sponge cake

Lemon cheesecake

Texture and temperature

All foods have texture, and we use words to describe how they feel in the mouth:

▷ Make a list of foods which could be described by the words above. Try to think of some foods which don't fit into these categories. Find words to describe them. ◁

We tend to expect foods to have a certain texture and usually avoid eating those with a different texture—lumpy custard, tough meat, dry bread. Nerve endings on the tongue, in the cheeks, and on the roof of the mouth send messages to the brain, which interprets the information.

The teeth are designed to break up food into smaller pieces and it is mixed with **saliva** (a watery substance produced in glands in the neck) which moistens the food, to make it easy to swallow.

▷ Try eating 3 plain cream crackers in 1 minute. What happens in your mouth? ◁

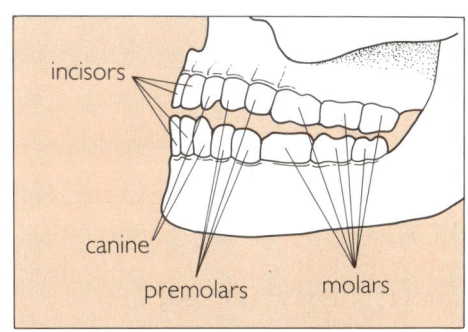

Cooking food often develops the flavour and changes the texture of it, and many foods are traditionally eaten hot or cold. For example stews are eaten hot and patés are eaten cold. If a food is too hot or too cold, its true flavour may be masked, and it may be uncomfortable to eat.

▷ **Things to do**

1 Collect some packaging, labels, or advertisements from foods, and describe how the manufacturer has tried to make the food look attractive.
2 Invent your own food product to sell, and draw a poster to advertise it. Put several on display and ask others to say which food appeals to them most, and why. Don't forget that the written description of the food is important as well as the visual description. ◁

Advertising

Advertisements are an important and effective way of persuading people to buy goods and services. Food manufacturers and shops spend large amounts of money every year to encourage us to buy their products, and they do so by various means, including television, radio, magazines, newspapers, posters and hoardings, and leaflets through the door.

All advertisements have to comply with the British Code of Advertising Practice, which sets out in detail the rules and regulations which advertisers must follow before their advertisements are made public. The general rules of the code are:

1 All advertisements must be legal, decent, honest, and truthful.
2 Advertisements should not in any way mislead the public about the product or advertiser.
3 Advertisements should show a sense of responsibility to people and society, for example they should not encourage violence or disregard safety.
4 All advertisements should conform to fair competition between different manufacturers and businesses.

The Advertising Standards Authority monitors all advertisements which appear in magazines, newspapers, cinemas, and on posters, and the Independent Broadcasting Authority monitors those which appear on television or radio. They can prevent advertisements from appearing if they do not comply with the code of practice. These authorities have no power over the advertisers themselves, but they can prevent an advertisement being published (being made public).

Many foods are advertised every year, particularly newly 'invented' ones, such as snack foods, or instant foods.

▷ **Things to do**

Conduct your own survey on food advertisements in the following way: (this could be carried out by a group)

1 Count and record the food advertisements (drinks too) that appear in the following:
  a television—over several days and at different times
  b independent radio—over several days
  c magazines and comics—several recent copies
  d posters and hoardings in a particular town
2 Compile two charts like the ones shown to demonstrate the following from your survey:
  a **category of food advertised**
     fresh e.g. milk, bread, meat
     snacks e.g. biscuits, crisps
     sweets
     meals, part or whole
     drinks, alcoholic
        and non-alcoholic
  b **group of people the advertisement was aimed at**
     parents of babies
     children
     teenagers
     adults
     all ages
3 Findings:
  a which was the most popular way of advertising foods in your survey?
  b which category of food was most commonly advertised?
  c which age group of people were most of the advertisements aimed at and why do you think this was so?
4 Why do you think that it is so important for food advertisements to conform to the code of practice?
5 Study a few food advertisements carefully, and try to decide in what way you are attracted to, or interested in, the product; is it:
   the colours used
   the description of the food
   the cost
   the situation the advertisement shows, e.g. a home, playground, sport? ◁

Food technology

Our food choice has been greatly increased by the work of scientists called **food technologists**. Food technology has become an important industry during this century and is still growing.

Food technology has five main functions:

1 To produce cheaper substitutes for basic foods; for example margarine was developed early this century as a substitute for butter. It is made mainly from vegetable oils, by a special process that causes the oils to become solid. Colourings, flavourings, vitamins A and D, and other substances are added to it to make it as similar to butter as possible. Margarines which remain soft even at low temperatures have been developed and are suitable for making cakes and other baked goods.

2 To increase food production by improving agricultural techniques; for example scientists have been able to develop varieties of cereals such as wheat and rice, that produce more seed per plant and are less likely to be affected by diseases and pests. This means that more food can be produced on the same amount of land.

3 To produce foods which can be prepared quickly (convenience foods). There are many foods that come into this category and they are popular because people now want to spend less time preparing foods than they used to.

4 To produce new types of food by artificial means; for example imitation cream is made from oils and other ingredients and can be used instead of real cream.

5 To preserve food for longer. This is important to cut down wastage and to make sure that food reaches customers in good condition. It is also important to preserve foods so that the consumer can store them longer—for example, frozen, dried, and canned foods.

About 95% of the food we eat today is prepared or treated (processed) in some way before we eat it.

Each year, many new food products are developed, and some of them (e.g. baked beans in tomato sauce, cornflakes) have become very popular and have been sold for many years.

▷ Things to do

1. Make a list of convenience foods, under the following headings:
   instant foods (very quickly prepared)
   frozen foods (need only thawing, or thawing then cooking)
   ready to eat foods (need no preparation)
   food mixes e.g. cake mixes (can be prepared and cooked quite quickly)
   canned foods that can be used as part of a meal or dish, such as pie fillings

2. Find out and either write about, or draw a poster of, the following methods of preserving food:
   canning   dehydrating (drying)
   ultra heat treatment   freezing

3. Soya beans are rich in protein, and new protein foods have been developed from them to make products that are similar in taste, texture, and colour to meat. Find out from books or leaflets about the products (available in many health food shops), how these foods are made and how they are used. If possible arrange a small tasting panel for meat, and meat substitutes mixed with meat. For example use minced beef made into bolognese sauce and compare it with meat mixed with soya granules (according to the directions on the packet) in the same recipe. Record people's reactions to the substitutes mixed with meat compared to their reactions to real meat.

4. Vegetable products are much cheaper than animal products (animals have to be reared and fed, sometimes for a few years, before they are killed). Therefore protein foods from plants are much more economical than those from animals.
   What other advantages can you think of for these new protein foods? Can you think of any disadvantages? ◁

Facilities for storing and preparing food

The kitchen has always been the centre of activity in the home, and many people spend a lot of time and money in planning their kitchens. Kitchens in many old houses were large rooms. Many had extra rooms alongside them, for example a pantry where food was stored and a scullery where other chores, such as cleaning, were carried out.

Kitchens in modern houses are usually much smaller, and may include an area for eating as well as a large variety of equipment.

How does the kitchen affect food choice?

Storage space The storage space in a kitchen will affect how much, and which types of food can be bought at one time. Older houses often had a special cupboard (a larder or pantry), which was usually cool and well ventilated, where food was stored and which sometimes had room to walk in. Modern houses tend not to have these, so food has to be stored in ordinary wall cupboards which are much smaller.

Refrigerators and freezers help people to store perishable foods (ones which 'go off' quickly) for longer periods of time, which is a great advantage.

Equipment for preparing food There are many pieces of kitchen equipment available to help people prepare food quickly and conveniently. Some are electrical, e.g. mixers, liquidisers, and microwave cookers, and many are mechanical (operated by hand), e.g. knives and pans.

Some equipment is specially designed to help disabled or elderly people with weak limbs, e.g. bottle and jar openers.

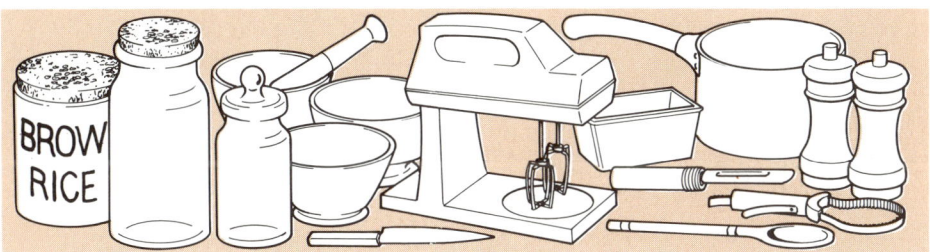

▷ **Things to do**

1 Make a list (you could illustrate it with pictures), of all the essential pieces of equipment you think would be needed by a small family, to prepare their meals. Look round some kitchen shops and in magazines to help you. Does the list surprise you?
2 Make a list of the minimum amount of equipment you would need to take away on a hiking and camping holiday, to prepare meals. Remember—you would have to carry everything!
3 What advantages are there in owning a refrigerator and freezer other than the one stated?
4 Where is the safest place to store heavy items of food such as cans?
5 How should you store dried foods to keep them in good condition?
6 Collect some leaflets and information on kitchen cupboards and units, and plan your own ideal kitchen on a piece of graph paper. Show where you would store your food, and which pieces of equipment you would choose. Give reasons for your choice, and also describe the colour scheme and decorations you would choose. If possible, work out how much your ideal kitchen would cost.
7 Look at the pictures of the kitchen equipment below, and find out what they are called, what they are used for, and which countries they come from. ◁

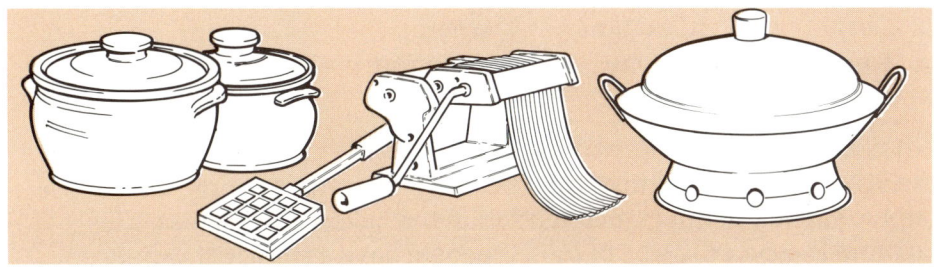

Part II

How food choice affects health

Food and health

What is a healthy person?

Healthy people usually have the following features:
   they are alert and have good reactions
   they are energetic and enjoy some physical activity
   they enjoy food and eat a good variety
   they have a good complexion and shiny hair
   they sleep well and relax easily
   they do not often suffer from illnesses

▷ There are many factors which affect our health. Some of these are listed below. Find out how and why each one can affect health: ◁

   sleep   relaxation   stress
   food   hygiene   pollution
   exercise   smoking   drugs

In most of the examples above, people are able to control the way in which each one influences their health, for example people can choose not to smoke, or how much relaxation they allow themselves. This control is especially true of food if people have a sufficient variety.

What does food consist of?

Have you ever considered what food contains, or what will happen to it once it has been swallowed?

Most foods are a mixture of a variety of different substances, such as:
   nutrients, colourings, flavourings, water, fibre, preservatives

Some of these are already present in the food when it is grown, others are added when it is processed or prepared to sell to the public.

The nutrients

The most important group of substances in the food we eat are the **nutrients**. These are the things that our bodies need to keep alive and stay healthy. Each type of nutrient has its own name. There are *five* types of nutrient:

   protein   vitamins
   fat   minerals
   carbohydrate

Some of these include several things, for example the minerals include iron, calcium, and fluoride, (among many others) and the vitamins include vitamin A, B group, C, D, E, and K. Each nutrient performs a special job in the body and is found in a variety of foods. There is a chart on pages 34 and 35 which shows this.

Most foods contain several different nutrients—milk, wholemeal flour, and eggs are good examples of this—refer to the chart on the next page.
▷ Can you think why such foods are very useful to the body? ◁

Some foods, however, contain only one or two nutrients, and on their own they are of little value to the body. Sugar and lard (fat) are examples of this.

▷ **Things to do**

   Find out the reasons for the following:
1 Teenage girls need extra iron.
2 Fluoride (a mineral) is valuable to children but not adults.
3 Children need more protein for their size than adults do. ◁

The nutrients

Nutrient name	Job in the body	Found in these foods
Protein	1 Enables the body to grow. 2 Repairs the body when it is damaged. 3 Gives the body some energy.	meat, fish, eggs, cheese, milk, peas, beans, bread, rice, wheat, maize, nuts
Fat	1 Gives the body energy which can be stored. 2 Protects vital organs such as the kidneys from injury. 3 Insulates the body.	butter, margarine, lard, vegetable oils and fats, suet, meat, oily fish, egg yolk, cheese, nuts, fried foods
Carbohydrate	1 Gives the body a quick supply of energy. 2 Helps the body to keep warm. 3 Supplies the body with fibre to help remove waste products.	sugar, sweets, cakes, cereals, bread, biscuits, potatoes, fruit, vegetables, syrup, honey, jam
Vitamin A	1 Enables the eyes to see in dim light. 2 Keeps the linings of the throat, air passages, digestive system, moist and healthy. 3 Keeps skin healthy. 4 Involved in body growth.	carrots, milk, margarine, butter, oily fish, maize, liver, kidney, egg yolk
B group vitamins (*there are several in the group*)	1 Involved in the chemical reactions that release energy from food. 2 Involved in body growth. 3 Keeps nerves, muscles, and blood healthy.	wholemeal bread, yeast extract, meat, pulses (peas, beans, lentils), milk, eggs, fish
Vitamin C	1 Helps bind the body cells together to make tissue. 2 Helps body absorb iron. 3 Helps to make blood. 4 Keeps skin healthy.	citrus fruits, potatoes, cabbage, peppers, brussels sprouts, fruit juices

Nutrient name	Job in the body	Found in these foods
Vitamin D	1 Enables the bones and teeth to grow properly. 2 Helps body absorb calcium and phosphorus.	margarine, butter, milk, egg yolk, cream vitamin D is produced in the body when it is exposed to sunshine
Calcium	1 With phosphorus it gives bones and teeth their hardness and strength. 2 Helps the blood to clot after an injury. 3 Helps muscles and nerves to work properly.	milk, cheese, bread, green vegetables, canned fish, pulses
Iron	1 It is important for carrying oxygen around the body in red blood cells.	meat, kidney, liver, heart, treacle, bread, chocolates, cocoa, curry powder
Sodium Potassium Chloride	1 All three maintain the correct salt concentration of body fluids.	meat, milk, vegetables, fruit, cheese, fish, nuts, table salt
Iodine	1 Is required to make a special hormone that helps to control the chemical processes in the body.	water, green vegetables, fish
Water (not strictly a nutrient but essential for life)	1 Essential for life. 2 Helps digestion and getting rid of waste products. 3 Lubricates all body joints and tissues.	fresh water, fruit, vegetables, milk, meat, fish

▷ Things to do

1 Write down a list of all the foods you ate yesterday, then look at the chart and try to work out which nutrients were in them. Do you think that you had a good mixture of foods and nutrients?
2 Study the labels on a variety of foods and note how many of them say which nutrients the food contains.
3 Design a poster to tell people how important it is to eat a mixture of different foods in order to obtain all the nutrients. ◁

Individual needs for food

Everyone has a **biological need** for food. Food is essential for life. If the body lacks food, it soon becomes weak and ill.

How much food do we need?

People vary in the amount of food they need for a variety of reasons:

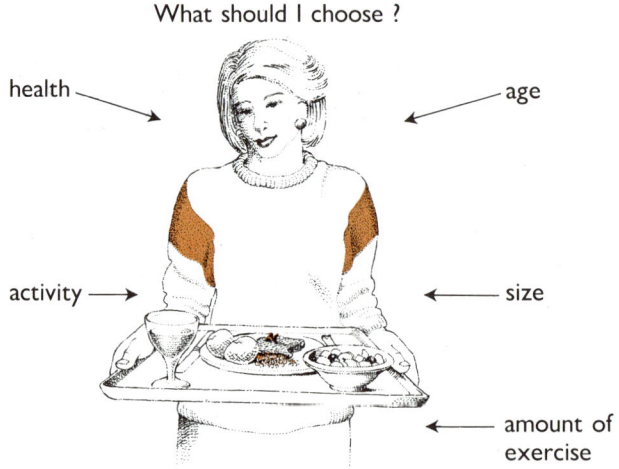

Age and size A person's requirements for different nutrients (see page 33) vary at different stages of their life. For example, babies and children need more protein for their size than adults, because they are growing rapidly. As people get older they often become less active, so need less food for energy. People vary in their height and the amount of muscle they have, which also affects how much food they may need.

Exercise and activity People who take regular exercise, e.g. running or swimming, need more energy from food than people who lead less active lives.

People who have active jobs, e.g. builders, labourers, or nurses, need more food to give them energy than those people with sedentary jobs (jobs that require little physical activity).

State of health If someone has been ill, in an accident, or has had an operation, food will be needed to repair and strengthen the body to bring it back to full health and fitness.

Pregnant women need extra nutrients to make sure that their baby grows and that they remain healthy throughout the pregnancy.

▷ Study the nutrients' chart on pages 34 and 35, and work out which nutrients would particularly be needed by:

a a person recovering from a broken leg
b a person recovering from an accident where they received a bad cut
Work out a day's meals for each one to include those nutrients. ◁

What foods should we choose to meet our needs?

Nutritionists can give people guidelines and advice about what is best for them to eat, in order to stay fit and well. A person who is able to eat a *mixture* of foods every day, is likely to be healthier than someone who has a very limited choice of food. This is because, the greater the variety of food available, the more chance the body has to receive all the nutrients it needs in the right quantities.

Most people in the UK have an interesting and varied choice of food, but unfortunately they do not always choose the best combination to keep them really healthy. This can lead to a variety of diseases like some of those on pages 48–55. It is advisable to try and choose some foods from each of the groups set out below, in everyday meals:

meat, fish, pulses, poultry   cereals and cereal based foods
fresh fruit and vegetables   milk, cheese, yogurt, eggs
fats and oils

▷ **Things to do**

Look at the meals below. Those in column A contain a good mixture of foods, and so would be of great value to the body. Those in column B are not as good, either because they contain too much of one type of food or lack others. For each of the meals in column B write down what is wrong (use the groups of food above and the nutrients' chart on pages 34 and 35 to help you), and say how you think the meals could be improved. ◁

A	B
Beef curry and rice Tomato and cucumber side salad Orange yogurt Water to drink	Sausage roll, chips Doughnut Orange squash
Egg and cheese flan Jacket potato Peas Fruit salad Milk	Pizza Spaghetti Chocolate ice cream Cola
Grilled fish Tomato, peas Creamed potato Fruit mousse Water	Lettuce, tomato, cucumber, cress 1 crispbread 1 apple Water

Dietary goals

Many doctors and nutritionists in the UK, USA, and other countries have been studying people's health and the ways in which their choice of food affects it.

It will become clear that there is much to be concerned about, but it should not be just the doctors and nutritionists who take the responsibility.

People cannot be made to eat only certain foods considered to be the most healthy for them—just think what it would be like if you had no freedom to choose what you would like to eat, and could only buy a very limited range of foods.

We do have a freedom of choice, but it is essential that we choose food that will keep us healthy throughout life.

How do you begin to make such an important choice? It is not easy—think back to all the factors which influence food choice.

▷ Try to put them in the order in which you think they influence you the most: ◁

history	likes and dislikes	health
beliefs and customs	the senses	facilities for storing
availability of food	advertising	and cooking food
cost of food	foods from other countries	technology

In 1983 several groups of people from organisations such as the Department of Health and Social Security, the Health Education Council, and the British Nutrition Foundation, published a report (called the NACNE report which stands for: National Advisory Committee on Nutrition Education) to try and help people make a sensible and healthy choice of food.

They have written their advice in the form of **dietary goals** which they hope people will aim for. Here they are:

Food labelling

Today, so many foods are pre-packed, that it would be difficult to know what they contained and to choose between them, if they were not labelled. Many foods in the UK have been labelled with a list of ingredients for some years. New EEC regulations came into force in 1983, giving consumers even more information, such as a date stamp to indicate when a food should be eaten by.

Now the information on a label is to be expanded even more, to include details about the contribution a food makes to health. The fat, sugar, salt, and fibre content of foods are to be listed on the label. For example, if there is more than 10% fat in a food, the manufacturer will have to state how much total fat there is, and how much of it is saturated and polyunsaturated (see page 43).

It is hoped that this information will enable people to make an informed choice when buying foods, so that they may meet the dietary goals that are recommended for good health.

Large supermarkets like Tesco are labelling foods for healthy eating with special signs. These foods also have a description identifying the particular benefit of the food to health.

Labels also give lists of additives, such as colourings, flavourings, and preservatives that are put into foods. These are often listed in code letters and numbers, such as E102 (tartrazine, which is a colour), and E220 (sulphur dioxide, which is a preservative). The Ministry of Agriculture, Fisheries, and Food issues a booklet which lists these additive codes and what they mean.

▷ **Things to do**

Study the labels on a variety of foods. List those which give the fat, sugar, salt, and fibre content, or make a point about the contribution their food makes to health, such as low sugar. Find out the meanings of the following words which are often seen on food labels:
  dextrose   stabiliser
  hydrogenated vegetable oil (or fat)   emulsifier
  flavour enhancer   antioxidant ◁

Thinking about sugar

In Britain, the average person eats 38 kg (84 lbs) of sugar a year, plus more in the form of glucose and honey. Much of that sugar is hidden in foods, so it is not always obvious how much is being eaten. The list below shows how much sugar is present in a variety of foods:

Food	Percentage of food that is sugar	Approximate amount of sugar in the given amount of food
50 g (2 oz) milk chocolate	45%	6 teaspoons
small tube boiled sweets	98%	10 teaspoons
1 tablespoon jam	68%	3 teaspoons
1 tablespoon peanut butter	3%	1 teaspoon
medium slice lemon meringue pie	22%	3 teaspoons
medium slice chocolate cake	26%	2 teaspoons
average can of cola	10%	7 teaspoons
1 carton (small) fruit yogurt	15%	4½ teaspoons
average chocolate biscuit	33%	2 teaspoons
small brick ice cream	15%	2 teaspoons
salad cream (3 teaspoons)	13%	½ teaspoon
sweet pickle (3 teaspoons)	25%	¾ teaspoon
drinking chocolate (3 teaspoons)	75%	2½ teaspoons
instant custard (1 packet)	38%	6¾ teaspoons
cornflakes (6 tablespoons)	8%	¼ teaspoon
dried chicken soup (1 packet)	10%	2 teaspoons
dried tomato soup (1 packet)	40%	8 teaspoons

If some of the figures surprised you, then you might well ask why is the sugar put into such foods?

It seems that the British have a great liking for the taste of sugar, and have come to expect many foods to have a sweet taste—even if it is only slight.

Sometimes sugar is put into foods as a preservative, to prevent the food from becoming spoiled by moulds and bacteria.

▷ Arrange a display of some of the foods listed above and invite people to estimate the amounts of sugar in each. Use this as part of a large display to make people more aware of the effects of sugar on their health.

Sometimes sugar is put into foods as a main ingredient and cannot easily be replaced with anything else. Cakes come into this group. Try to think of some more. ◁

In many cases though, sugar is added to foods which don't really need it to satisfy our desire for sweetness. This desire often starts at an early age.

Babies may be given foods sweetened by their parents, who do not like the flavour without sugar. However, babies do not need sugar and will enjoy the unsweetened, natural flavours of foods as they are gradually introduced to them.

Various reports have been prepared by the Government telling parents how babies should be fed to keep them healthy. One of their main concerns is about the amount of sugar given to babies, and they advise the following:

1 Sugar should not be added to bottled milk.
2 Sugar should not be added to solid foods.
3 Dummies should not be dipped in sugar, syrup, or honey to comfort a baby.

Baby-food manufacturers have responded to the recommendations in the reports in a variety of ways, such as not adding sugar to solid foods, and reducing the sugar content of foods like rusks.

Why worry about sugar?

Our bodies need **energy** in order to work properly. Sugar is a very good source of energy, so it does have a useful purpose. However, unlike most other foods, sugar does not contain any other nutrients, so it is of limited use to the body. We can get energy from other foods too, such as meat, fruit, vegetables, cereals, and many others, so there is no need to eat pure sugar.

Too much sugar can have bad effects on health. It is a main cause of tooth decay (see page 54). If it is not all used up for energy, then the left over sugar is changed into fat, which is stored under the skin. This can result in a person becoming overweight.

Sugar has a very intense flavour and can mask the true flavours of other foods, many of which are naturally sweet but to a lesser extent. Once the tongue becomes used to a particular level of sweetness, it becomes hard to enjoy anything less.

What should you do about the amount of sugar you eat?

▷ 1 Keep a record of all the foods and drinks you have over the next week, and make a list of those which contained sugar and those to which you added sugar, or syrup. Take a critical look at your list.
2 Try to work out where you could cut down on the amount of sugar you have eaten.
3 Try some foods, such as breakfast cereals or fruits, to which you usually add sugar, on their own, and compare their sweetness.
4 If you normally eat sweet snacks, try some savoury ones for a change such as cheese flavoured biscuits, savoury corn snacks. ◁

Thinking about fat

Fat is found in many foods, and is either liquid (oil) or solid. Some foods, for example lard, suet, butter, margarine, and vegetable oil are composed almost entirely of fat. Other foods contain 'hidden' fat—i.e. fat that is not obvious but nevertheless forms a large part of the food. Examples are cakes, crisps, biscuits, chips, sausages, chocolate, ice cream.

Why worry about fat?

Fat is an important nutrient to the body for several reasons:

1 It provides the body with a supply of energy. Any spare can be stored under the skin for later use.
2 Foods containing fat often also supply the body with vitamins A, D, E, and K.
3 Fat helps to make food palatable and easy to swallow.

Recently there has been much publicity about fat, because research has pointed to a link between the amount and type of fat that we eat in different foods and heart disease (see page 50). It is recommended that people should cut down on the amount of fat and change the types of fat they eat in order to lessen the risk of getting heart disease.

Foods containing fat

Fats are called **saturated** or **polyunsaturated** (see page 43). It is suggested that fats which are mostly polyunsaturated are better for health than those which are mostly saturated.

Polyunsaturated fats are mostly found in plants, for example sunflower, soya, and corn (maize) oils and margarines are made from them.

Saturated fats are mostly found in animal fats such as meat, butter, cream, cheese, lard, and suet.

Hydrolysed fats are fats which have been converted from saturated to polyunsaturated.

Hydrogenated fats are oils which have been converted from polyunsaturated to saturated, which makes them solid.

Some people do not think that there is enough evidence to support the view that cutting down on the amount of fat eaten reduces the risk of heart disease as there are so many other factors to take into account, so it can be very confusing for us to know what to do for the best.

It is not practical or sensible to cut fat out of your food choice altogether, so it is perhaps best to reduce the amount eaten, particularly if you eat a lot of fatty foods, and to use polyunsaturated fats in place of saturated ones where possible.

How could you cut down on your fat intake?

Here are some suggestions:

1 Spread butter, margarine etc., more thinly on bread and biscuits.
2 Try grilling foods such as sausages, fish fingers, beefburgers, bacon, chops etc., instead of frying them.
3 If you are fond of chips and would find it hard to give them up, try using chips which are baked in the oven instead of being fried, or try baked potatoes for a change.
4 When cooking, try using low fat yogurt instead of cream in items such as cheesecakes (try low fat cheeses too) and mousses (saves money too!).

▷ Things to do

1 List some other ways of cutting down your fat intake.
2 Look around some food shops and make a list of the products available which have had the fat content specially reduced, such as dairy products. Are they more expensive to buy?
3 Make a list of other foods, other than those on page 42, which contain hidden fat. ◁

Thinking about fibre

The word **fibre** is used in several different ways—fabrics are made from textile fibres and you can buy glass fibre. In food, the word fibre (its full name is **dietary fibre**) is used to describe the parts of plant foods that humans cannot digest. This means that the fibrous parts are not broken down in the body after they have been eaten. Plants make this fibre as part of their structure:

>the husks of seeds—e.g. cereal grains (wheat, oats, rice etc.), pulses (peas, beans, lentils)
>the skins and flesh of fruit—e.g. plums, apples, bananas, oranges etc.
>the leaves and stems—e.g. green leafy vegetables, rhubarb, celery, etc.

Foods which are made from any of these, for example wholemeal bread, celery soup, and bean stew, will contain fibre.

Why worry about fibre?

The body has to get rid of waste products from the food we eat, in order to stay in healthy working order. If it did not, it would gradually become poisoned. Liquid waste (**urine**) is made in the kidneys, stored in the bladder, and passes out of the body at regular intervals. Solid waste (**faeces**) is made in the intestines, and passes out of the body via the anus, at intervals which are different for every person. In order for them to be disposed of easily, the faeces must be soft and bulky. Fibre absorbs water as it passes through the body and this helps make the faeces soft and bulky.

If people do not eat enough fibre, then the faeces take much longer to pass through the body, because they become hard and compact. They are also much more difficult to expel from the body. This can lead to a variety of intestinal problems (see page 55).

Foods that contain fibre tend to be more bulky, and so make you feel full after a meal. This can be useful if someone is trying to cut down the amount of food they eat, as the fibre fills them up and should stop them over-eating.

Foods containing fibre

Many foods, for example white flour, white bread, white rice, and instant puddings are refined. This means that a large amount of fibre in them was removed when they were processed in a factory, so that the food is easy to prepare (cooks more quickly) and is easier to eat (more palatable).

Grinding wheat to produce flour

How to increase your fibre intake

1 Eat more fresh fruit and vegetables, perhaps particularly during snack times.
2 Try wheatmeal or wholemeal bread for a change, instead of white bread.
3 When baking, mix some wholemeal flour with white flour for cakes, biscuits, and pastries.
4 Try wholemeal pasta and rice, which are cooked in the same way as pasta made from white flour and polished rice, but may take longer.

▷ **Things to do**

1 Make a detailed list of foods available in shops where the manufacturer has added fibre or advertises the product as being high in fibre.
2 Compare the cost of these foods with similar ones which do not have added fibre. Why is there a difference?
3 Find out why whole grain cereals are better for you than refined ones apart from in their fibre content. ◁

Thinking about salt

Salt is found naturally in foods such as fish and meat. It is also added to many foods, for example cheese, bacon, and yeast extract, as a flavouring and to preserve them.

Salt has always been an important substance, and people used to trade for goods with it. The word **salary** (the money people earn in a job) comes from the salt money that used to be paid to Roman soldiers.

Why worry about salt?

Salt is needed by the body to keep all its fluids at the correct concentration. If people eat a mixture of foods, they should not need extra salt, unless they work in very hot places where they would lose salt in their sweat. However, most people like the taste of salt and use it every day in meals.

For some people, too much salt may cause their blood pressure (see page 50) to rise. This may affect the heart, kidneys, and other organs in the body. Too much salt is particularly bad for young babies, as their kidneys are too small to cope with the strain salt puts on them. Some baby food manufacturers have reduced the amount of salt in their products for this reason.

Nutritionists recommend that everyone should cut down on the amount of salt they eat, to reduce the risk of high blood pressure.

How can you reduce your salt intake?

1. Do not add salt to the water when cooking vegetables.
2. Study the labels on foods such as snacks and biscuits, and try those which have little or no salt added.
3. Try putting less salt onto food at mealtimes.

▷ **Things to do**

1. Find out why it was that salt was such an important substance for centuries.
2. It is possible to buy salt substitutes that do not contain **sodium** which is what causes the problems. Try to look at the label of one of these and write down what it contains. Note the price too.
3. Find out what happens to a person in a hot climate if they do not have enough salt. ◁

Thinking about alcohol

Many people drink alcohol (in beer, wines, and spirits) for social and festive reasons. A small amount of alcohol has the effect of reducing stress and tension, helping people relax, and making them feel more at ease with one another.

Why worry about alcohol?

An occasional alcoholic drink does not have a bad effect on the body. However, problems arise when people drink too much too often, and many people are affected and become dependent on alcohol and very ill. Alcohol affects the body in various ways:

1 It reduces the ability to concentrate and judge accurately things like speed, and distance. This is very dangerous if someone tries to drive a car or use a piece of machinery.
2 It damages the liver. The liver has to process the alcohol to prevent it being poisonous to the body, and too much, too often, can permanently damage the liver cells. This eventually results in a condition called **cirrhosis**, and can lead to death.

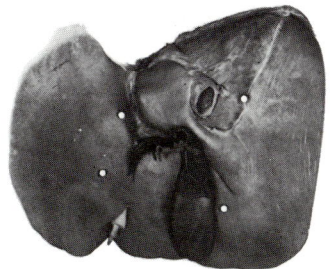
A healthy liver

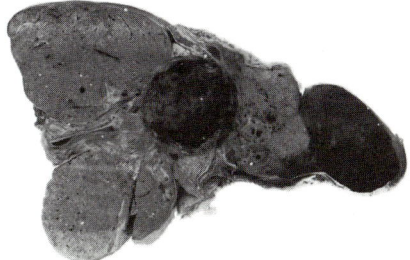
A liver with cirrhosis

3 It can affect the heart, by gradually poisoning it, and eventually making it fail to work.
4 If insufficient food is eaten, then the muscles and nerves become weakened and very sensitive.

Sadly, there are many people of all ages who are alcoholics (they are dependent on alcohol), and it is a very difficult condition to get over. It can cause families to break up and much unhappiness all round.

▷ **Things to do**

1 Find out some information about the work of Alcoholics Anonymous and how they go about helping people with an alcohol problem.
2 Why is it important that there are strict punishments for people who drink and drive? ◁

Heart disease

More than one quarter of all deaths in the UK are caused by heart disease. It mainly affects middle aged people. Heart disease is a major problem in other countries too, such as the USA, Finland, and Norway. There are many different types of heart disease, the most common being **coronary heart disease** (CHD), which eventually results in heart attacks.

The heart

The heart is made of muscle and acts as a pump. It contracts about 70 times a minute, if the person is resting, and this motion pumps blood through blood vessels to the lungs to collect oxygen, and then to all parts of the body. This means that the body is continually supplied with vital substances such as **oxygen** and **nutrients**. The heart muscle needs oxygen to work, and gets this from the blood in the **coronary arteries**. The heart has to work continually from the time before a baby is born until a person dies. That is why it is so important to keep it healthy.

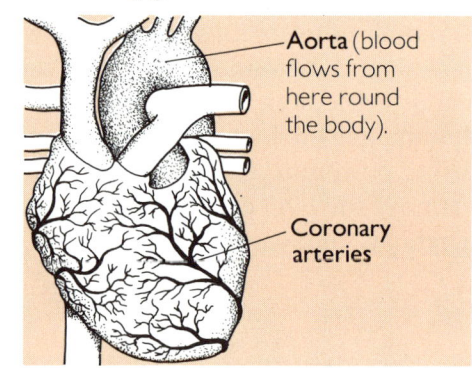

What happens in heart disease?

The coronary arteries which supply vital oxygen to the heart, are like tiny pipes. If they become blocked with fatty deposits (called **atheroma**) then the blood carrying oxygen cannot reach the heart so easily—it may be prevented from doing so altogether. This is coronary heart disease.

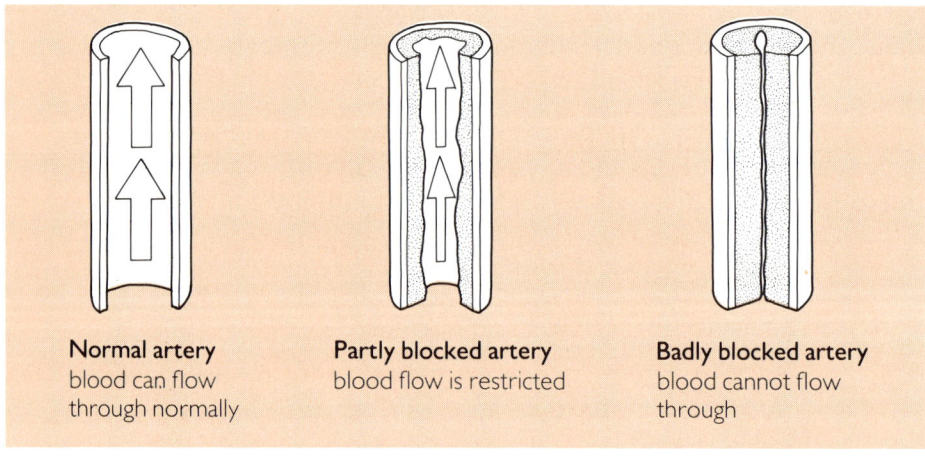

Normal artery blood can flow through normally

Partly blocked artery blood flow is restricted

Badly blocked artery blood cannot flow through

What are the symptoms of heart disease?

If the arteries become blocked, not enough blood will get through and the heart muscle will be starved of oxygen. This will cause a sharp, cramp-like pain across the chest, down the left arm and around the neck. This is called **angina**. It is often associated with exercise and usually disappears after rest.

However, if there is a sudden and complete blockage in the arteries so that no blood and therefore no oxygen can reach the heart muscle, then the person will suffer a **heart attack**. They will have severe pain in the chest, neck, and arms which will not disappear for several hours. They may feel sick and faint. The attack badly damages part of the heart, so that afterwards it is weaker.

Sometimes the heart may stop beating altogether during a heart attack, and this is called a **cardiac arrest**. Unless the person receives emergency first aid to revive them within a few minutes, they will die.

▷ You may know someone who has had a heart attack. If possible, ask them to describe what happened, how they felt during and after the attack, what treatment they had, and how they have to look after themselves now. ◁

What causes heart disease?

Because heart disease is such a major cause of illness and death, there has been a lot of research carried out to try and find the causes and how to prevent it. The types of food we eat is known to be important, and it has become clear that there are several factors which can all lead to heart disease. They are:

- food
- lack of exercise
- being overweight
- age
- heredity
- high blood pressure
- stress
- smoking

Food

This factor is one which has caused much discussion, research, and controversy. It is well known that if people eat too much food, particularly starchy, sugary, or fatty foods, they are likely to become overweight, which will put extra strain on the heart. There is also evidence to show that eating too many of certain types of foods, particularly **fatty foods**, can increase the risk of heart disease.

Cholesterol is a substance that is absorbed by the body from the fat we eat. The body also makes cholesterol in the liver. If a person eats a lot of fat, then the amount of cholesterol in the blood is likely to be high.

Cholesterol is known to speed up the blocking of the coronary arteries, especially if there is an excessive amount in the blood. So there is a greater risk of heart disease in people who eat too many fatty foods.

The fats in food are said to be either **saturated** or **polyunsaturated** (see page 43). These words are used to describe the molecules of fat. It is suggested that **saturated fats** are more likely to increase the cholesterol level in the blood, and so therefore people should reduce the amount of saturated fat they eat. Page 43 shows which foods contain saturated fats.

Too much salt is also unhealthy as it may increase the blood pressure in some people.

High blood pressure

The heart pumps blood through the blood vessels at a certain pressure to make sure it reaches all parts of the body. The pressure occasionally increases, when the heart beats faster, to allow more blood to get to the brain and muscles more quickly at certain times, for example when exercising or when under stress. It should then fall again to a steady resting level.

Some people have a constantly high blood pressure, so that their heart has to work harder all the time. This seems to increase the risk of developing coronary heart disease. High blood pressure may be inherited or may be related to several things such as, being overweight, smoking, drinking too much alcohol, eating too much salt.

▷ How is blood pressure measured? If you have the chance, ask a doctor or nurse to take your blood pressure—it doesn't hurt!—and record your result. ◁

Lack of exercise

Exercise helps to strengthen the heart and other muscles, as well as relieving stress and making a person look and feel fitter. Lack of exercise is unhealthy as it may lead to a person being overweight, and to the heart becoming sluggish. If a person takes up regular exercise, they should gradually increase the amount they do to prevent undue strain on the heart.

▷ Write down the type and amount of exercise that you do regularly. Why do schools have compulsory physical education lessons? How could you increase your exercise if you don't do much? ◁

Overweight

Being overweight puts extra strain on the heart. It has to pump blood harder as the muscles have to cope with moving extra weight around.

Overweight people are more likely to suffer from high blood pressure too.

Heredity

Heart disease may affect several members of a family, because they have inherited a tendency to get it. However, it does not mean that all members of a family will suffer.

Age

The older a person is, the more likely they are to suffer from heart disease. However, the damage to the coronary arteries can begin at a young age, which means that the care of the heart should start in childhood, rather than waiting until it is too late and the damage is done. Men appear to be more likely to suffer from heart disease, but older women are equally at risk.

Smoking

Smoking cigarettes can **double** the risk of a person dying from heart disease, and in particular, they may die at a young age.

Cigarette smoke contains several substances, including **carbon monoxide** and **nicotine**. Carbon monoxide reduces the amount of oxygen that can be carried in the blood, and therefore reduces the amount that reaches the heart. Nicotine causes the blood pressure to rise, which puts a strain on the heart. Also, the coronary arteries become blocked up more quickly in those people who smoke.

▷ Apart from the risk of heart disease, in what other ways does smoking affect people's health and their appearance? ◁

Stress

Stress can be brought about by several factors, such as personal, family or money problems, pressure at work, anxiety, and worry. A certain amount of stress in every day life is quite normal. However, if a person is constantly under stress they may not relax enough. This may cause the blood pressure to rise, which may lead to a heart attack in some people.

▷ **Things to do**

1 Write down any stresses you have in the next two days, for example, being late, arguing, forgetting to do something, and suggest how you could avoid them in the future.
2 List all the ways in which you could reduce the possibility of developing heart disease, and those which you can do nothing about. ◁

Being overweight

Being overweight is a very common problem for people in countries where there is no shortage of food, such as the UK. It causes much misery and illness and affects people of all ages. When the body weight becomes excessive, so that it is dangerous to health, the person is said to be **obese**.

Various charts have been produced for people to check their weight against their height, to see if they are overweight. The charts below are examples. Charts are generally produced for adults; children and teenagers are growing rapidly, so it is difficult to give meaningful figures for them.

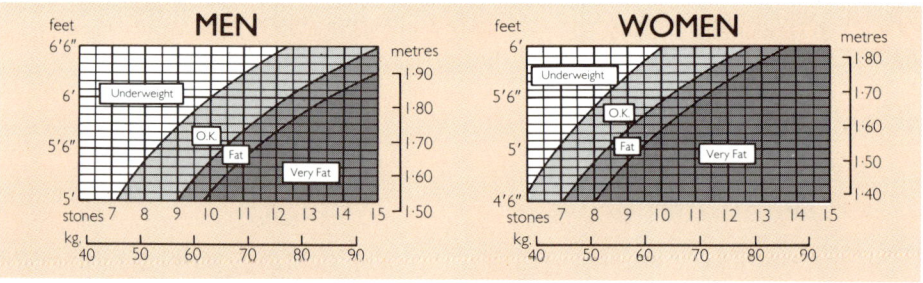

It should be remembered that the figures are averages. People do vary in the amount of muscle they have and the size of their bones, both of which can affect weight. The charts often give ideal weights for three frame sizes of the same height. The size of a person's frame; small, medium or large, is the size of their bones.

How is weight put on?

If a person eats more food than their body needs, i.e. it does not use up all the energy, the extra is turned into fat and is stored under the skin in special cells called **adipose tissue**. The extra fat can build up over weeks and months if a person continues to eat too much.

Why do people eat more than they need?

Hunger is controlled by a special part of the brain called the **hypothallamus**, which 'tells' the body when and how much to eat. It does this by sensing how full the stomach is, what the body temperature is, and how much sugar there is in the blood. Unlike most wild animals, which rely on this system to tell them when to eat, humans are also influenced by outside factors. The sight or smell of food can encourage us to eat, even though we may not actually need more food at that time. A lot of people eat if they are bored. Being with people who are eating a lot can also encourage us to overeat. With all these outside influences, and the fact that food is so readily available for most people in this country, it is easy to see why overeating is a common problem.

How does being overweight affect health?

Being overweight can create emotional and physical problems.

Emotional problems Overweight people are often unhappy about their appearance. They may have difficulty in finding fashionable clothes to fit them. They may be teased and ridiculed by other people. This can lead to a vicious circle, where the overweight person turns to food for comfort, which in turn increases the problem.

Physical problems Extra weight puts a strain on the bones and joints—particularly those which support the weight, such as knees, feet, and hips. Extra fat around the chest may lead to breathing problems and to an increased risk of illnesses such as bronchitis.

Blood pressure often increases and the heart therefore has to work harder, which puts a strain on it (see page 50).

The risk of having an accident also increases, because overweight people are unable to move quickly to avoid risky situations.

Losing weight Many overweight people try to lose weight by following a slimming diet. Popular magazines often have suggestions to help people slim, and there are many slimming aids such as special foods and exercise equipment for sale.

It takes time and strong will power to lose weight effectively, and people often give up because they find the diet too hard or monotonous to follow.

If someone diets too strictly, they may lose too much weight and become weak and ill. They may become obsessive about dieting and not realise that they are making themselves ill. This condition is called **anorexia nervosa**, and is quite common, particularly in teenage girls in countries where there is plenty of food. Some people have died because of this; the treatment is long and needs patience and understanding by all concerned.

▷ **Things to do**

1 Find out about and write a short account about any local and national organisations (e.g. Weight Watchers) which try to help people lose weight. Find out how they do this and how many people come to them for help.
2 Make a list of slimming aids that you see advertised for sale, and find out what they cost. Do you think they would be helpful? Why? ◁

Dental disease and intestinal disease

What happens in dental disease?

Humans have two main sets of teeth—the first set (deciduous or milk teeth) are shed in childhood, and the second set are meant to last for the rest of one's life.

After a meal, food, especially sweet sticky food, is left on the teeth. Bacteria which live in the mouth combine with these food deposits and form **plaque**. If it is not removed by regular cleaning of the teeth, the plaque builds up, especially where the teeth join the gums and on the biting surfaces of the teeth.

Gum disease may be caused by irritating substances produced by the bacteria as they feed on the sugary deposits. The gums become sore and infected as a result (called **gingivitis**), and the tissues which support the teeth may weaken and lead to a loss of teeth (called **peridontitis**).

Tooth decay is the result of the breakdown of sugar by the bacteria. As they do so, the bacteria produce **acids** which attack the enamel surface of the tooth and gradually cause its destruction. This is how it happens:

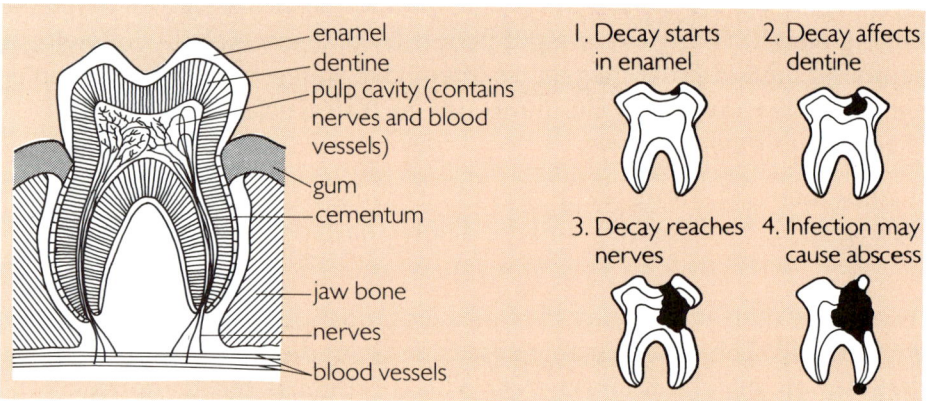

Why is food choice so important to prevent dental disease?

The more sugar a person eats, the more contact it will have with the teeth, and the more likely the teeth are to decay. Foods that have sugar added to them, e.g. sweets, cakes, biscuits, soft drinks, jams, jellies, and many others, are a main cause of the problem. It is therefore advisable to reduce the amount of such foods in the diet, as well as making sure that the teeth are properly cleaned and cared for.

Teeth are made mainly from calcium and phosphorus, so it is wise to include foods such as milk, cheese, pulses, bread, and fish that contain those minerals in your food choice.

Intestinal disease

There are a variety of intestinal diseases, and many people are sufferers.

A major cause of some of these is that people do not eat enough fibre in their food (see page 44). Lack of exercise is also partly to blame, as exercise helps to keep the intestines active. Two of the most common intestinal diseases are constipation and diverticular disease.

Constipation When people are constipated, they have great difficulty in getting rid of solid waste products, **faeces**, from their body. Their faeces become very hard and compact, due to lack of fibre to keep them soft and bulky. Discomfort is felt in the abdomen, and much effort is required to get rid of the faeces. Many people suffer from this condition, which is best treated by increasing the fibre intake in food.

Diverticular disease If someone is constipated, the walls of their intestines have to work hard to move the faeces along. The lining of the intestine may become weak in places because of this extra strain. Little pouches (called **diverticula**) of the lining may be forced out through the wall of the intestine. These may become infected and very painful. The disease can be treated in the early stages with a high fibre diet, but if it gets very bad, then the patient may have to undergo surgery to remove the affected part of the intestine.

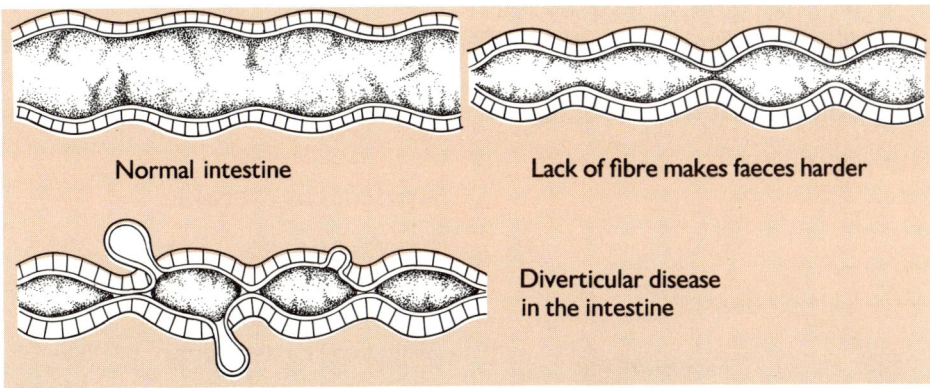

Normal intestine

Lack of fibre makes faeces harder

Diverticular disease in the intestine

▷ **Things to do**

1 Find out why fluoride is put into some brands of toothpaste and into the water supply in some areas of the country.
2 What are plaque disclosing tablets and how can they help people to look after their teeth?
3 On your next visit to the dentist, ask your dentist what treatments are available to help prevent tooth decay.
4 Many people take laxatives if they become constipated. Find out how these work, and say why it is not a good idea to rely on laxatives all the time. ◁

Low sugar recipes

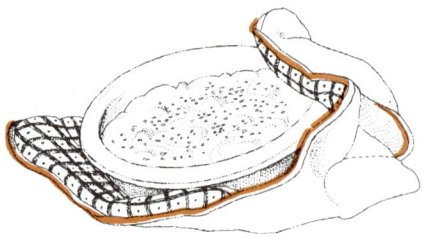

Coconut fruit crisp

Ingredients
2 egg yolks
150 g (5 oz) plain or fruit yogurt
2 ripe pears or eating apples
25 g (1 oz) desiccated coconut

Method
1. Peel, core, and roughly chop fruit.
2. Mix egg yolks with yogurt.
3. Stir in fruit.
4. Place mixture in medium sized oven-proof dish, and bake at gas 4/180°C for 30 minutes until set.
5. In last 5 minutes of cooking time, sprinkle coconut over the top.

Spiced fruit pudding

Ingredients
75 g (3 oz) fresh breadcrumbs
2 eggs, separated
275 ml (½ pint) skimmed milk
1½ tsp mixed spice (ground)
25 g (1 oz) dried fruit

Method
1. Place breadcrumbs in a 2 pint oven-proof dish.
2. Beat egg yolks with milk, stir in spice, and pour over breadcrumbs.
3. Add dried fruit, and mix well together.
4. Leave to stand for 10 minutes.
5. Whisk egg whites until stiff, and fold carefully into mixture.
6. Bake at gas 4/180°C for 40 minutes until golden brown.

Apricot cheesecake

Ingredients
small can apricots, in natural juice
2 eggs
25 g (1 oz) caster sugar
grated rind and juice of ½ a lemon
100 g (4 oz) cottage cheese
150 ml (¼ pint) natural yogurt
12.5 g (½ oz) plain flour

Method
1. Grease and line the base of a 15 cm (6″) round cake tin.
2. Drain fruit and save juice.
3. Sieve or liquidize the cottage cheese.
4. Beat eggs, and add rest of ingredients, mixing well.

5 Pour into tin and bake at gas 4/ 180°C for 30 minutes.
6 Leave to cool slightly, then remove carefully from tin.
7 Arrange fruit neatly on top.
8 Serve warm, with the juice — which could be thickened with cornflour or arrowroot to make a sauce.
9 Other fruits, e.g. peaches or pineapple could be used.

Lemon mousse

Ingredients
2 eggs—separated
1 large or 2 small lemons
a few drops liquid sweetener
12.5 g (½ oz) gelatine
275 ml (½ pint) natural yogurt

Method
1 Grate rind of lemon finely.
2 Beat yolks, sweetener, and lemon rind together.
3 Dissolve gelatine in 2 tbsp water in a bowl over hot water.
4 Stir gelatine and lemon juice into mixture.
5 Stir in yogurt.
6 Whisk egg whites until stiff and fold carefully into mixture.
7 Leave in a cool place to set and decorate with grated chocolate, lemon slices or nuts.

Low sugar rock cakes

Ingredients
225 g (8 oz) self raising flour
75 g (3 oz) margarine
25 g (1 oz) sugar
100 g (4 oz) dried fruit
1 egg
1–2 tbsp milk

Method
1 Sieve flour, and rub in margarine until mixture becomes like breadcrumbs.
2 Stir in sugar and fruit.
3 Beat egg and stir in with milk until a stiff mixture is formed.
4 Place small rocky piles of mixture onto a greased baking tray.
5 Bake at gas 5/190°C for 20–25 minutes until golden brown and set.

Low fat recipes

Caribbean chicken—serves 3–4

Ingredients
225 g (½ lb) cooked chicken (cut into small cubes)
¼ cucumber—chopped into cubes
small piece red pepper—cut into small pieces
small tin pineapple pieces in natural juice (drained)
60 ml (⅛ pint) low calorie salad dressing
150 ml (¼ pint) natural low fat yogurt

Method
1 Combine all ingredients thoroughly in a bowl, except pineapple juice.
2 Chill in refrigerator.
3 Serve with a green salad.
4 Garnish with tomato or lemon slices if required.

Tuna curry rice—serves 4–6

Ingredients
small can tuna fish in brine (not oil)—broken up with a fork
¼ cucumber—chopped into cubes
1 medium red eating apple—sliced and dipped in lemon juice
175 g (6 oz) cooked long grain rice (cold)
150 ml (¼ pint) low calorie salad dressing
150 ml (¼ pint) natural low fat yogurt
2–3 level tsp curry powder

Method
1 Combine all ingredients thoroughly in a bowl.
2 Chill in refrigerator.
3 Serve with a green salad and crusty bread.

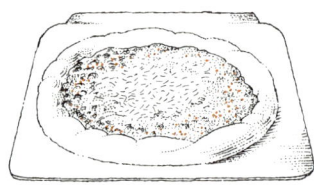

Low fat pizza—serves 2

Ingredients
100 g (4 oz) self raising flour
12.5 g (½ oz) margarine
60 ml (⅛ pint) skimmed milk
1 small can tomatoes—drained and chopped
1 small onion—finely chopped
pinch mixed dried herbs
50–75 g (2–3 oz) low fat cheddar cheese—grated

Method
1 Rub margarine into flour until mixture is like breadcrumbs.

2 Add milk and mix to a soft elastic dough.
3 Roll out into a 20 cm (8") diameter circle and place on a greased baking tray.
4 Place onions, tomatoes, and herbs onto dough. Sprinkle cheese on last.
5 Bake at gas 7/220°C for 20–25 minutes until golden brown on top and well risen.

cheese—run machine until the mixture is smooth.
4 Dissolve gelatine in water in a small bowl over a pan of boiling water.
5 Add to mixture and mix well.
6 Whisk egg white until stiff.
7 Fold into mixture, pour into flan case, and leave to set.

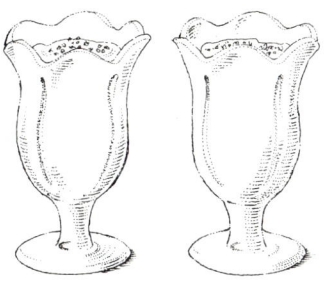

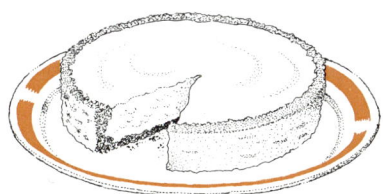

Lemon Cheesecake

Ingredients
6 digestive biscuits—crushed
50 g (2 oz) low fat spread — melted
150 ml (¼ pint) natural low fat yogurt
100 g (4 oz) cottage cheese (plain)
1 egg—separated into white and yolk
25–50 g (1–2 oz) sugar
1 lemon
12.5 g (½ oz) gelatine
2 tbsp water

Method
1 Mix biscuit crumbs and margarine together, and press into base of a 17.5 cm (7") plain flan ring on a baking tray. Chill.
2 Mix sugar and egg yolk together, and add yogurt, lemon juice, and finely grated lemon rind.
3 Either sieve cottage cheese and add to mixture, or place mixture in a liquidizer and add cottage

Yogurt and fruit whip
serves 2–3

Ingredients
225 g (8 oz) fruit—e.g. bananas, strawberries, oranges or apricots
1 tbsp honey
275 ml (½ pint) natural low fat yogurt
a few chopped nuts to decorate

Method
1 Peel the oranges or bananas.
2 Chop fruit up into small pieces.
3 Place all ingredients except nuts into a liquidizer and run for 30 seconds until mixture is smooth.
4 Pour mixture into individual dishes and chill in refrigerator.
5 Decorate with nuts.

High Fibre recipes

Savoury crumble—serves 4

Ingredients
225 g (8 oz) wholemeal flour
100 g (4 oz) margarine
75 g (3 oz) grated cheddar cheese
(or low fat cheddar cheese)
Sauce:
25 g (1 oz) margarine
25 g (1 oz) flour
275 ml (½ pint) low fat milk
350 g (¾ lb) mixed vegetables—e.g. onions, potatoes, carrots, beans, peas
salt and pepper

Method
1 Cook chopped vegetables in boiling water until tender. Drain.
2 Sauce—melt margarine, add flour and cook gently for 1 minute. Remove pan from heat, and add milk slowly, mixing well until smooth. Heat, stirring constantly until sauce has boiled and thickened. Add salt and pepper. Add mixed vegetables.
3 Crumble—rub margarine into flour, and stir in grated cheese.
4 Place sauce mixture into ovenproof dish and spread crumble mixture carefully on top.
5 Bake at gas 6/200°C for 20–25 minutes until crisp and golden on top.

Fruit crumble—serves 4

Ingredients
175 g (6 oz) wholemeal flour
50 g (2 oz) porridge oats
75 g (3 oz) sugar
100 g (4 oz) margarine
350 g (¾ lb) stewed fruit, e.g. apples, plums, apricots, blackberries, damsons or rhubarb

Method
1 Rub margarine into flour until like fine breadcrumbs.
2 Stir in oats and sugar.
3 Place fruit in ovenproof dish. Carefully spread crumble mixture on top.
4 Bake at gas 6/200°C for 20 minutes, until crisp on top.

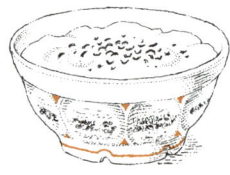

Apple Charlotte—serves 3–4

Ingredients
350 g (¾ lb) stewed apple
225 g (8 oz) wholemeal breadcrumbs
75 g (3 oz) margarine
75 g (3 oz) demerara sugar or less if preferred
150 ml (¼ pint) natural low fat yogurt
grated plain chocolate to decorate

Method
1 Gently fry breadcrumbs in margarine until crisp.
2 Remove from heat, add sugar, and leave to cool.
3 Put alternate layers of apple and breadcrumbs in a dish.
4 Pour the yogurt on top and decorate with chocolate.

Lentil soup—serves 3–4

Ingredients
100 g (4 oz) lentils—either brown or orange
1 medium onion
1 chicken stock cube
1 medium carrot
1 stick celery (optional)
seasoning

Method
1 Chop the onion, carrot, and celery into small pieces.
2 Place all the ingredients in a pan with 575 ml (1 pint) stock.
3 Bring to the boil and simmer for 15–20 minutes until all the vegetables are tender.
4 Liquidize the soup and season to taste.
5 Serve with wholemeal rolls or scones.

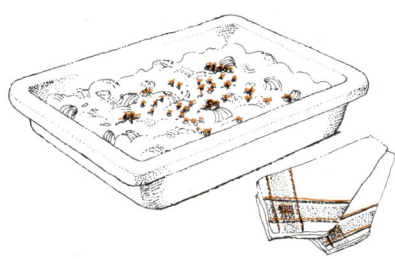

Pasta neapolitan—serves 4

Ingredients
225 g (8 oz) wholewheat pasta, e.g. shells
1 medium onion, finely chopped
2 tbsp oil
1 medium can tomatoes
grated rind and juice of 1 lemon
1 tbsp tomato puree
2 tsps caster sugar (optional)
salt and pepper

Method
1 Boil the pasta until tender in plenty of water.
2 Fry the onion in the oil until transparent.
3 Add the rest of the ingredients, and simmer for 10 minutes, breaking the tomatoes down with a spoon as they cook.
4 Pour the sauce over the pasta in an ovenproof dish.
5 Serve with grated cheese or chopped parsley.

Quiz
What sort of food chooser are you?

Read the ten questions below, and choose one of the answers in each case. Answer them truthfully, and think about them before you do.

At the end, add up your score from the chart on page 64, and see which category of food chooser you fit into.

1 It is breaktime at school and you are hungry. Which of the following snacks would you choose to eat?
  A crisps
  B chocolate bar
  C an apple
2 Do you eat three meals a day without eating in between?
  A never
  B always
  C sometimes
3 It is lunchtime. You are offered a choice of potato to go with a meal of chicken pie, peas, and carrots. Which would you choose?
  A jacket (baked)
  B instant mashed
  C chips
4 You have just received some pocket money. What would you choose to spend it on?
  A drinks from the vending machine
  B entertainment
  C sweets
5 Do you ever experiment and try out new foods?
  A sometimes
  B often
  C never
6 Do you add sugar to hot drinks?
  A always
  B never
  C sometimes
7 You are left in charge of cooking the evening meal, which includes sausages. How would you cook

the sausages, bearing in mind that the meal also includes chips?
A bake them
B fry them
C grill them

8 You have the choice of the following puddings to go with a meal of beef curry, rice, carrots, and peas. Which would you choose?
A instant fruit flavoured milk pudding
B fruit yogurt
C doughnut

9 You are going out for the day. Which of the following packed lunches would you choose?
A cheese sandwiches (white bread), packet of crisps, chocolate biscuit, squash to drink
B cold fried sausages, packet of crisps, chocolate bar, doughnut, cola to drink
C wholemeal cheese sandwiches, piece of fruit cake, orange or apple, fruit juice (unsweetened) to drink

10 Which breakfast would you choose from the following?
A a drink of tea only
B glass of fruit juice, poached egg, wholemeal toast with marmalade or savoury spread
C bowl of sugar coated corn flakes, milk, grilled sausages and bacon

How did you score? (See page 64.)

31–40 Good choices generally. You have chosen a good variety.
16–30 Not bad. Go easy a bit on your sugar and fat intake.
 8–15 Oh dear! You are getting too much sugar and fat compared to the other nutrients you are eating, and you are not eating enough fibre.

Index

additives 33, 39
advertisements 26–27
Advertising Standards Authority 26–27
age 36, 51
alcohol 47
angina 49
anorexia nervosa 53
atheroma 48

babies 41, 46
blood pressure 46, 50, 53

cash crops 15
cholesterol 49, 50
constipation 55
convenience foods 9, 28
coronary heart disease (CHD) 48
crops 5, 15, 16
crop destruction 16

decorations (food) 24
dental disease 54
dietary fibre 39, 44–45
dietary goals 38
disease 16, 37
drought 16

energy 41, 42, 52
exercise 32, 36, 50

famine 16, 17
fat 37, 39, 41, 42–43, 49, 53
fibre – see dietary fibre
food 33, 49
  availability 12–13
  cost 18–19
  distribution 7, 13
  festivities 10–11
  labelling 39
  preservation 28, 40
  processing 28–29, 45
  production 6, 17
  rationing 13, 16
  shortage 12, 16–17
  storage 30–31
  technology 7, 28–29
garnishes 24
gum disease 54

halal 11

health 32, 36, 38, 39, 52, 53
heart 46, 47, 48
heart disease 42, 43, 48–51
hidden fat 42, 43

importing food 8, 12
intestinal disease 44, 55
irrigation 16

kitchen 30–31
kosher foods 10

likes and dislikes 20–21

margarine 28
menus 20–21

nutrients 33, 34–35

overeating 53
overweight 41, 50–51, 52–53

plaque 54
polyunsaturated fat 42, 43, 50
population 17
poverty 16

rationing 12–13, 16
refined foods 45
religious beliefs 10–11

salt 39, 46, 50
saturated fat 42, 43, 50
saving money on food 19
sense organs 22–25
sight 24
smell 22, 23
smoking 32, 51
staple foods 14–15
stress 32, 51
sugar 39, 40–41, 54
supermarkets 12

taste 22, 23
teeth 25, 41, 54
texture 25
tooth decay 41, 54
traditional foods 8

war 15–16
weight charts 52

Answers to Quiz on page 62

		Question									
		1	2	3	4	5	6	7	8	9	10
	A	2	1	3	2	2	0	2	2	3	1
Score	B	1	5	2	4	3	5	1	4	1	4
	C	4	3	1	0	1	2	3	1	5	2